COLLAGE
FUNDAMENTALS

COLLAGE
FUNDAMENTALS

TWO- AND THREE-DIMENSIONAL TECHNIQUES FOR ILLUSTRATION AND ADVERTISING

By

Oscar Liebman

STRAVON EDUCATIONAL PRESS
New York, N.Y.

To my wife Mildred, severest of critics, but always constructive and supportive, this book is dedicated with love.

Library of Congress Cataloging in Publication Data

Liebman, Oscar, 1918-
    Collage fundamentals.

    Includes index.
    1. Collage—Technique.   I. Title.
N7433.7.L53   702'.8   79—262
ISBN 0—87396—079—3

Printed in the United States of America

CONTENTS

PUBLISHER'S
ACKNOWLEDGEMENTS

Editor   Don Stacy
Copy Editor   Elvin Abeles

The publisher wishes to thank the following people for their help in furnishing permissions and reproduction material necessary to produce this book: Claudia Bismark of the Museum of Modern Art, Irene Moore of the Philadelphia Museum of Art, Jeffrey Bergen of the ACA Galleries, Murray Bates of Continental Oil Company, Roy Mayers and Bob Shipman of Globe Book Company, Inc., William H. Dowse of Eastern Air Lines Incorporated, Ken Hines and Kenneth Rhine of Caldwell Communications, Bernie White of *Argosy*, Dale W. Phillips of Fawcett Publications, Ian Summers of Ballantine Books, Inc., Rosemary Frank of Time/Life, Henry Epstein of ABC Television, Paul Back of *Newsday*, Morris D. Dettman of Honeywell Information Systems Inc., Gail Swerling of Sonnabend Gallery Inc., Joseph Comiskey of Benzinger Bros., George Pertuzzo of Grossett & Dunlop, Al Catalano of A.T. & T.

LIST OF ILLUSTRATIONS

INTRODUCTION

THE USE OF COLLAGE, MIXED MEDIA, AND THREE-DIMENSIONAL COMPOSITIONS is relatively new in the field of commercial art.

Whether used singly or in combination, these techniques represent a vast expansion of possibilities to the creative illustrator. Each artist can now explore a whole world of textures and materials that, in the past, would have had to be drawn and painted by hand. Instead of this time-consuming work, the materials are used in themselves. The artist is free to act as a skillful editor-producer, and the whole world becomes filled with stage props. If an old worn and stained wood panel is beautiful, it no longer has to be painstakingly copied; it can be used just as it is.

A lot of control is needed to create a two- or three-dimensional collage despite the fact that drawing in itself can almost be eliminated. Of course, a subtly arranged composition made of varied colored papers that is used as a background for a beautifully executed line drawing expands the impact of sheer draftsmanship. Yet many artists who excel at collage lean more towards a tactile approach. Rather than worrying about sketching a profile of a head, for example, they conceive of the image in material forms. A peach-colored sheet of paper is cut out as a profile with scissors or a matt knife. Then an eye is cut from a photograph and pasted in place. The mouth can be from another photo or cut from a vivid red piece of paper and laid in position. The hair can be from wallpaper or made from a yellow fuzzy cord piled up and glued down.

In the above case it is not a question of drawing or not drawing, it is simply the exercise of a more sculptural attitude, one that deals in physical properties.

Another artist may bond a photo to a sheet of plywood and skillfully cut it out with a jigsaw. The edge of the wood could be painted in white, or in a color, and the whole thing stood up against or nailed onto a contrasting colored ground. Here real light and shade are part of the original conception. In the long run drawing as a form in itself is only one point of view among other viewpoints.

The illustrations and suggestions given in this book are meant to increase the reader's visual vocabulary. It is not a question of step-by-step lessons or of final solutions. They are really a shared experience based upon the work of over 30 years as a professional illustrator. Each individual artist must find his or her own creative path. I would like simply to introduce new methods and demonstrate concretely how they can be used in the commercial field.

There is no one way for the creative artist. I am always learning, and each job I undertake leads me to new possibilities.

If I can communicate the excitement and joy to be found in this work and encourage young artists to experiment with these forms and become fine collagists, I will be more than happy.

The illustrations in this book were chosen to represent a wide selection of technical range. It was impossible to include every great illustration. I extend my gratitude to each publishing house, advertising agency, and artist who gave permission to reproduce the work that is used.

Start your own collection of collage illustrations. Study them and use them as a base and inspiration for your own work. No one creates from nothing, so don't hesitate to look, learn, and do.

A BRIEF
HISTORY

THE MOST MODERN OF TECHNIQUES IS ROOTED IN EF-
FORTS OF THE PAST. This applies to collage and its three-
dimensional relatives.

Art began as such an integral part of life that it was not thought
of as "Art," much less categorized as "Fine" or "Commercial."

A short survey may well aid in placing these "new" ideas into
a perspective that connects them to human history.

The use of letters of the alphabet as a cultural form has a long
history. In ancient China characters were carved in stone and
rubbings were made to transfer them to paper. Calligraphy, the art
of brush writing, is still considered in the Far East to be a higher
art than painting. In Iran, where pictorial images are prohibited by
religion, the Kufic script is made into a marvelous decorative form
that is used to decorate architecture, pottery, and even fabrics.
The pages of manuscripts, such as the famous Celtic *Book of Kells*,
combine letters and figurative painting in a beautiful manner.
Letters are found carved on monuments of all kinds from prehis-
toric glyphs to Egyptian and Roman inscriptions. The illusion of
carved letters is also found in Renaissance painting. It gives a
sculptural appearance to the architectural scene and can present
an apt Biblical quotation. Albrecht Dürer often signed his work
with his initials appearing as though carved into stone.

Since the present day environment is crowded with signs of

11

COLLAGE ON GLASS   (Artist unknown)   Collection, Art Wiethas

all types, letters and words are used in art as a symbol of contemporary culture. Signs *are* the Times! Artists such as Paul Klee built paintings around words and letters.

Like many art terms, *collage* is a French word, and means merely "pasting." (*Colle* is the word for paste or glue, and *coller* means the act of pasting or glueing.) The technique first called *papier collé,* "pasted paper," is now generally known under the more general term, *collage*. The French word *assemblage*, meaning a "collection," is used for a compostion made of actual objects often also known as a "construction." *Montage*, or "putting together," and *découpage*, "cutting out," both refer to covering things with cut-up photos, prints, or materials. Max Ernst called some of his works *frottage*, which means "rubbing."

OBJECT (Roses des vents)   *Joseph Cornell*   Wooden box with twenty-one compasses set into a wooden tray resting on plexiglass-topped and partitioned section, divided into seventeen compartments containing small miscellaneous objects and three-part hinged lid covered inside with parts of maps of New Guinea and Australia   Collection, The Museum of Modern Art, New York (Mr. and Mrs. Gerald Murphy Fund)

NATURE MORTE   Georges *Braque*   Paper and drawing   Permission, Los Angeles County Museum of Art

Folk art of all kinds has used pasted images on objects to decorate them. For an early modern example, Dutch artists of the 16th century placed actual butterflies on paintings of flowers. Collage in its contemporary sense began around 1912 with Pablo Picasso (1881-1973), Georges Braque (1882-1963), Juan Gris (1887-1927), and Kurt Schwitters (1887-1948). Rather than imitate a decorated wall, the artist used a piece of real wallpaper. For pictures of collages by Gris and Schwitters see the color plates on pages 17 and 18.

Jean Dubuffet (1901-   ) dripped and blotted paint on canvas, then cut out interesting patterns, and reassembled them into strange landscapes and figures.

Max Ernst (1891-1976) would place paper over a rough grained wood surface and by rubbing with a stick of graphite pick up the pattern of the raised grain. He also rubbed over ordinary objects. A comb rubbing became the back and ribs of a surrealistic horselike creature.

As far as the use of three-dimensional materials is concerned, masks and sculpture from Africa and the South Seas contain feathers, bones, shells, and even nails.

Picasso mixed sand with paint in order to create texture, or glued it down in its natural color to form a beach. In sculpture he used odd pieces of wood, forks, toy cars, all kinds of unexpected things. A large basket became the rib cage of a goat. When a bicycle seat was crowned with handlebars it became the head of a bull!

Objet trouvé, another French term, means "found object." Picasso once picked up (found) a small blunt piece of twig. He made the shape of an ash tray in clay, placed the wooden stump on it, and it turned into the remnants of a cigar!

"Ready-made" is another category, and is used for things that are not transformed or changed into a visual pun, but are left just as they are. Marcel Duchamp (1887-1968) placed a porcelain urinal in an exhibition. Of course, it created a great shock, since the object was completely out of place, but as a gesture against the art establishment it was quite successful.

The French sculptor César (Baldaccini) (1920-   ) chose scrap metal from old cars and had them pressed into three-dimensional statements about modern times.

In America, Joseph Cornell (1901-1974) created boxlike constructions as stage settings for his favorite images and personal fantasies. Some of today's most successful commercial collagists have been influenced by Cornell's art. Robert Rauschenberg (1925-   ) introduced a combination of objects and paintings to express an anti-aesthetic position; and Edward Kienholz (1927-   ) recreated entire rooms in an attempt to reproduce what he conceived as the chaos and decadence of contemporary society.

Illustration is also a reflection of present-day values. At least it must remain free to choose from the history of man in order to find a means of communication that works in today's society.

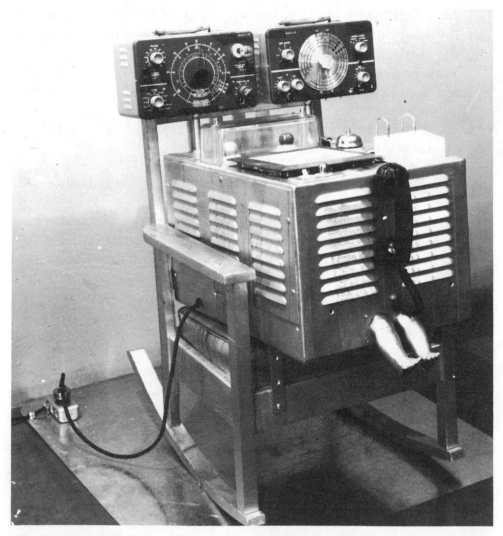

THE FRIENDLY GREY COMPUTER — STAR GAUGE MODEL *Edward Kienholz* Motor-driven assemblage: aluminum painted rocking chair, metal case, two instrument boxes with dials, plastic case containing yellow and blue lights, panel with numbers, bell, "rocker switch," pack of index cards, directions for operation, light switch, telephone receiver, doll's legs, 40 x 39⅛ x 24½ on aluminum sheet 48⅛ x 36   Collection, The Museum of Modern Art, New York (Gift of Jean and Howard Lipman)

STILL LIFE — THE TABLE *Juan Gris* Pasted paper, printed matter, charcoal, and gouache on paper mounted on canvas Permission, Philadelphia Museum of Art (The A. E. Gallatin Collection)

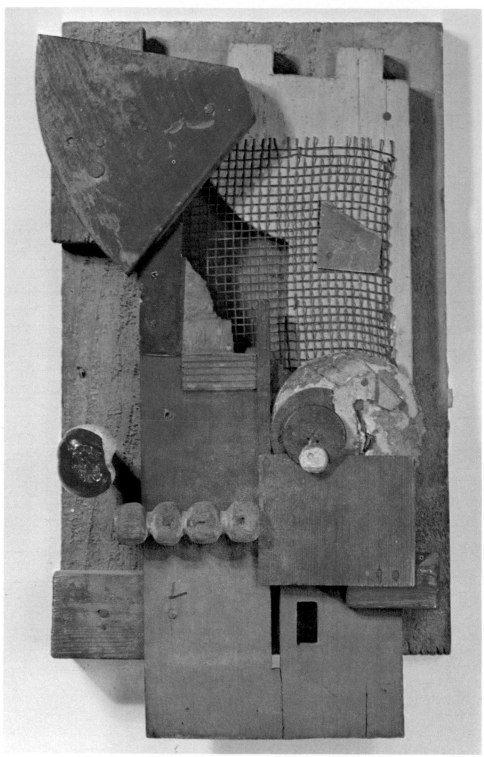

MERZ KONSTRUKTION *Kurt Schwitters* Pasted paper, wire, and paper
Permission, Philadelphia Museum of Art (The A. E. Gallatin Collection)

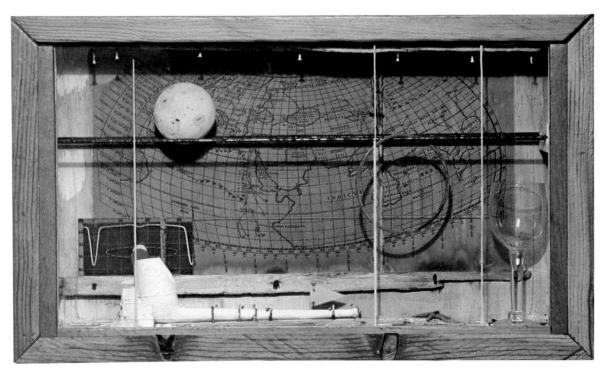

SOAP BUBBLE VARIANT   *Joseph Cornell*   Box construction   Permission, The ACA Gallery

FLEMISH CHILD   *Joseph Cornell*   Box construction
Permission, The ACA Gallery

CANYON   *Robert Rauschenberg*   Combination of mixed media   (Private collection, New York)

MATERIALS AND SOURCES

TWO- AND THREE-DIMENSIONAL COLLAGES are made by cutting, tearing, building, arranging, and painting. *Any* object is potentially useful. Collect everything that might lend itself to artistic expression. Stamps, coins, photos of movie stars and important people, of crowds, costumes, papers of varied color and texture, plastic bits, graffiti, all can be used.

A great many interesting objects can be found in attics, cellars, garages, junk shops, and even city dumps. Search through toy departments, cut-rate stores, flea markets, garage sales, as well as your house or apartment. Many mementos and souvenirs that are old, torn, and discolored with age become transformed when introduced into a collage. It is as though they are given new life as these images reach out of the past to play a role in our time. This category also includes old picture postcards, pieces of bridal veil or lace, pressed flowers, dolls, newspapers with headlines that announce an important event, baby shoes, birth certificates, engravings, even tools. Anything that is half forgotten and hidden away can be brought to light and reactivated by this new technique.

Paper

Paper products include cardboard, corrugated paper, all kinds of printed material from magazines, matchbook covers,

OBJECTS FOR COLLAGE   (Created by the author as an illustration for this chapter)

"1776" (detail of a collage for a book jacket)   *Oscar Liebman*   Pasted parts of reproductions of historical documents, photographs, campaign button, and three-dimensional plastic numerals   Permission, Globe Book Co.

PAPER COLLAGE   *Oscar Liebman*   Pasted theatre ticket stubs, news headline, photograph, and miscellaneous bits of paper (Created by the author for this chapter to illustrate the use of paper in collage)

wine and spirit labels, theater and sports tickets, posters, snap-shots, baggage stubs, and so on.

As far as quality is concerned, some papers, such as colored construction paper, have a tendency to fade and fall apart. Most commercially made paper has high acidity. In the manufacturing process, acids are added to help disintegrate the pulp to make it into a souplike mixture that will finally solidify into paper. The problem is that the acid continues to break down the fibers throughout the life of the paper. In addition to this difficulty, most colors are made of dyes that are not light-fast. For colored paper to be permanent, a low-acid paper would have to be stained, sprayed, or painted with artist's colors. Test various papers out before using them. Check whether the colors will run or if the paper tends to dissolve when wet.

Introducing printed paper into a collage may create some practical problems. For example, when glueing paper that is printed on both sides, the damp coat of glue may cause the underside to show through and thus interfere with the selected image. Glue should be used sparingly, but if this effect is desired in order to soften the impact of the image, it can be forced to happen by spraying the surface with clear acrylic while the glue is still wet. This works best with thin or absorbent paper such as newsprint.

Ink on a slick, heavily coated paper can be made to move or "bleed" if turpentine or lacquer thinner is rubbed over it. The fumes of the thinner are not healthy, so the less it is used the better.

Paper can be toughened and made waterproof if a coat of acrylic medium is brushed over it. This gives it a protective coating and a slight shine which deepens the colors. Over this coat colors can be added. If a thin layer of paint is used without the addition of white, it becomes a colored stain called a glaze.

By glazing over paper and printed matter with color the whole can be made uniform. Parts that tend to jump out can be quieted, or, through the addition of color, an important area can be made to stand out with emphasis.

Finding paper is easy. There are hundreds of different papers, from those made commercially to wonderful hand-made papers from all over the world. Most art-supply stores carry a surprisingly large variety of paper.

Write to paper companies asking about their products. They are usually generous in sending samples; moreover, as a new paper comes out, you will be on their mailing list. Write to the Paper Makers Advertising Association for a list of paper manufacturers. The address is 90 Elm Street, Westfield, Massachusetts 01085. They also publish a magazine called *The Printing Paper Quarterly* which is devoted to the use of paper in the graphic arts.

It is good to be in contact with these large companies. They often make use of commercial artists to test products. Well-known illustrators are used for advertising and promotion jobs. Keep this in mind as a potential market.

Cloth

Cloth is an excellent material for use in collage. It has endless variations of pattern and many textures. Lace creates a delicate feeling, while burlap has a course masculine quality. Wool cloth,

CLOTH COLLAGE *Oscar Liebman* Combination of assorted bits and strips of cloth pasted around picture of woman's face (Created by the author for this chapter to illustrate the use of cloth in collage)

WOOD ABSTRACTION *Oscar Liebman* Strips of different woods to illustrate the use of wood in collage (Created by the author for this chapter)

however, is difficult to use because it soaks up too much glue, becomes limp, and completely loses all character. A white or solid-colored cloth can be formed into wrinkled surfaces that can be shaped into facelike forms or made into undulating hills and valleys as in a landscape. It can be mounted on a panel and glued in just those areas where it needs to be secured, or the whole piece can be dipped in acrylic medium, shaped, and left to dry on the background surface. Cloths of different textures can be torn, ripped, or cut into strips and laid over one another to build up designed shapes or to play one pattern against another. Thin window-curtain material that has some transparency can be used to veil an overstrong element in the composition.

Once the cloth is cemented down and given a spray of clear acrylic, it can be painted to change its color. An image can also be created *on* the cloth as well as *by* it.

Because of its great flexibility, cloth is an important material for pulling together the separate units in the design of the collage.

Wood

Wood and wooden objects are indispensable for collage. Collect old furniture parts, ornamental moldings from broken picture frames, carved parts of doors and cabinets, knobs and handles of all kinds, children's blocks, and parts of toys. Ordinary pieces of wood that have clearly defined grain and knots are good to use. Driftwood or old stained slabs that have been aged and given character by the weather are also very beautiful.

Since the grain is the hard part of the wood, it can be greatly enhanced if it is wet and rubbed with a wire brush. Brush *with* the grain. This removes some of the softer pulp and makes the tougher grain lines stand out in relief.

Like the other materials, wood can also be stained and painted. If it has a rich quality of its own, try not to cover this over. Use transparent colors or stains that allow the character of the wood to show through. Wood that is ordinary can be painted and then sanded or wire brushed. This will create an antique type of finish.

Using a coping saw or a jigsaw, specific shapes can be cut out and assembled. Wood can also be cut into or carved. Use softer woods for carving until you have gained experience.

Constructions can be made that are actually three-dimensional sculptured objects.

Look at wooden sculpture and increase your understanding and appreciation of this lovely material. Think of the old cigar-store Indians along with the masks from the South Sea Islands or Africa, and find some reproductions of the large wooden figures done by the English artist Henry Moore (1898-   ).

Metal

Metal is another material that is filled with possibilities for collage. Think of nails, tools, kitchen utensils, clock parts, plumbing pipes and joints, toilet balls, coins, automobile parts, motor gears, and so on. An old sewing machine is filled with unusual and exciting parts. Old lead soldiers and toy cars are wonderful in their place.

Aside from the various kinds of metal, from polished steel or chrome to brass, its artistic quality is increased by age — for example, the green patina of copper, a metallic gleam showing through a worn, half-painted surface, and even rusted parts give color and the feeling of time.

METAL ABSTRACTION *Oscar Liebman* Construction to illustrate the use of metal in collage (Created by the author for this chapter)

To secure metal, a strong glue, such as an epoxy resin type, is needed. Some items can be nailed or screwed down and of course with special training can be soldered and welded.

There are pressure-sensitive tapes of metal that can be used. Copper and brass can be bought in thin sheets and can be cut into strips or shapes to be bent or even curled without difficulty.

It is especially exciting to transform a pile of metal junk into an entirely new form.

Plastic

One of the most modern materials to be developed is plastic. Since this material comes in many colors and patterns it is a very useful collage item. It comes in sheets of various thicknesses, tubing, spheres of all sizes, and cylinders. Sheet plastic is malleable enough to mold into forms of your own. When heated, the plastic sheet can be gently curved or bent. Once it cools it will keep the new shape. Electric heating strips for bending plastic are available, but a hot soldering iron can be run down the edge of a metal ruler until the plastic softens enough to be bent. Tubing can be formed by heating it in a hair curling iron. Some artists shape or wrinkle the plastic pieces by immersing them in boiling water.

Plastic can be cut rather easily with a saw or, if it is scored with a sharp edged tool, it will snap in two without effort.

Faces and figures made of tubing are a good way to introduce sculptural effects to a design.

Of course, ready-made flowers, forks, spoons, cups, and similar products should be collected for their potential use. The bright color of plastic objects gives them eye-catching importance. Plastic is easy to glue to the board or to itself.

Natural Objects

Nature is filled to abundance with material for collage. These natural objects include sand, shells, pebbles that are highly polished by the sea, weathered rocks, flowers, plants, leaves, and feathers. The more fragile things can be protected by coating them with acrylic medium.

I have placed real objects gathered from nature next to a photographic reproduction of the same subject. This creates a strange other-dimensional image, a kind of visual "double take."

Pictorial Material

It can be difficult to find specific material that is needed for a collage when you are facing a deadline.

DOUBLE TAKE   *Oscar Liebman*   Arrangement of natural objects against a photograph of similar objects (Created by the author for this chapter)

As far as pictorial images are concerned, most libraries have picture collections. These are filed and indexed according to subject matter. Once you find what you are looking for, have it photocopied to whatever size is needed.

There are also special services that supply old and new photographs as well as prints, engravings, posters, and visual material of all kinds. There is a charge for this service, but they will make a duplicate from any material to fit your requirements. If you have trouble finding a company of this kind, look in the directory called *The Literary Market Place* under "Photo and Picture Sources." Once you make contact with this type of service, keep their catalog handy. It is an invaluable source and next best to having your own pictorial archive. Remember, they carry just about every image that you can imagine. If you need a picture of a movie star of the 1920's, a figure from history, a special type of factory, something to do with medicine, animals, types of transportation, or historical places, you will find it here.

Max Ernst, a pioneer in collage techniques, cut up old engravings and reassembled them to make wild and even shocking pictures. Look up his works; it's a good inspiration.

Start your own file system of pictures. Place them in folders and catalog them. I have one for historical subjects, portraits, costumes, landscapes, and so on. It saves a lot of time if you can put your hands on what you need without leaving the studio.

When using photographic material, try not to use the entire picture. This would be leaning too heavily on someone else's work. Just tear or cut parts of it so that when it is used with other things and colored or toned to fit the composition, it becomes your own expression. Each work should reflect your personality as if it were your handwriting.

All these ideas about materials and their uses are merely hints — small attempts to share some of the excitement that still catches me each time I work.

Texture

Chipped paint and dried acrylic paint can be glued down to form strange textures. When modeling paste is applied in a thick layer, many fine cracks appear. Once the paste is dry, these cracks are permanent, and they can be stained to form very interesting surfaces.

Texture is not just something to use in collage; it is also something to collect. As billboards, exterior posters, and advertising become old and ravaged by time and weather, remove and save them. They become deposits of fascinating multicolored textures for use in some future collage illustration. Don't think of yourself as a scavenger but rather as a collector of elements of a future masterpiece.

A letter, parts of a word or image, a buildup of many layers of ads can produce a mine of potential material.

Try to think texturally. Imagine a group of marbles with window screening thrown over them! With practice this aspect of the new vocabulary will further expand your creative abilities.

Surfaces

A variety of surfaces can be used as a base for collage — for example, wood panels, masonite, and illustration board. If objects are chosen that are heavy, then a thicker base should be used.

Masonite is most versatile. It is a pressed wood panel that

comes in four-by-eight-foot sheets. It is easily cut and is quite durable when coated. Use the untempered kind that is light in color. The darker sheets have been treated with oil to temper them against the weather; this added oil is not a good surface for acrylic paint or glue.

Be careful about surface warping. It is best to give the back a good coat of medium to offset all the glue added to the front. Next, prime the front with two or three coats of acrylic gesso, alternating the direction of the brush strokes with each coat. A paint roller can also be used. If a really smooth surface is desired use fine sandpaper or steel wool on the gesso when it is dry and hard.

Adhesives

A transparent glue with good adhesive power is basic to collage. The white glues like Elmers are good but they are not as waterproof when dry as is acrylic medium. Acrylic also comes in different consistencies. The heaviest is called gel and is rather like toothpaste. Modeling paste is gel with the addition of marble dust or a similar filler; this dries in a white, hard form that can be carved and sanded.

Epoxy glues come in two parts which must be mixed with care in order to insure proper drying. They are best for heavy objects.

Contact cements are fine, but they must be used with care, since they bond on contact and cannot be moved around. Rubber cement is an exception to this, for thinner can be run under the glued area, which can be lifted up and repositioned. It is quite handy for paper work, especially if time is limited. It will cause a yellow stain to form on the paper with time, so it should be used only when necessary.

I use acrylic medium for the most part. It is a very good bonding agent, as you can tell each time you try to open the jar! It also forms a waterproof protective film of plastic over everything.

Tools

Be sure to have a variety of sharp-edged cutting tools; single-edged razors, matt knives, carving tools, gouges, shears, and various types of saws are all valuable.

Power tools such as a drill, a small jigsaw, or a flexible shaft can make many jobs more simple.

A variety of brushes is important. I use a large bristle brush, about three inches wide, for applying gesso. Varied widths of flat sables are needed for glazing and fine pointed brushes are good for retouching or adding details.

TOOLS OF THE ART *Oscar Liebman* Line drawing to illustrate subtitle "Tools" of this chapter

The Studio

Use as large a work surface as possible. Unlike artists who draw and paint, a collagist requires a great amount of space for materials and tools. The studio is part shop, not just a place for an easel.

There is really no end to things that lend themselves to collage. Every common object can be used. Buttons, pipe cleaners, string, plastic containers, Styrofoam packing, colored glass and plastic, old dolls, tin cans, dried-out paint brushes, palettes, and all sorts of manufactured products are usable. I have a corner in my studio filled with old frames, broken-down plumbing fixtures, and all kinds of unwanted odds and ends waiting to be converted to art.

Storing all these items is a problem, for a good deal of space is needed. Place things in clearly labeled boxes and, if possible, keep them within sight of your work table. Just looking at some of these things can inspire a composition.

Good light is important. If daylight is out of the question, use the fine artificial lights on the market. Fluorescent and incandescent bulbs will affect the way color looks. The first makes everything look cool, while the second gives a yellowish cast.

Color-corrected bulbs can be obtained for fluorescent lights and are worth having. Otherwise a slight glaze can be added to the work to put the color back in balance.

Care of Work

Many early collages have fallen apart with age because the artists did not use the right materials or did not have the most recent technical advantages. Choose your materials with care.

Acrylic colors are made of permanent pigments, but many markers and colored inks are made from dyes that are not light-fast. If a coloring material is permanent, the manufacturer is sure to say so. Coating the finished work with acrylic medium, as I've said before, gives it a hard but flexible covering that does protect delicate papers as well as objects. No coating, however, keeps out light, so beware of colors that fade. Using good materials may not always be called for, but it is worthwhile to get into the habit of considering *all* your work of value.

Nevertheless, since time is often a factor in doing illustration, it can help a lot to use transparent colored acetate sheets. They have a pressure-sensitive adhesive backing and are colored to match standard printing inks. These can be placed over photos, newspaper and magazine clippings, or any paper work instead of using paint. They give a smooth, uniform tone without leaving brush marks, and they reproduce well. The value or strength of the color on these sheets is given in percentages. There is a 15-percent or a 60-percent value, for example; 100-percent is the strongest amount of each color.

Since one sheet of color can be placed over another the effect is the same as applying glazes.

If small, torn colored shapes of acetate are spread over the surface, slightly overlapping one another, a beautiful stained-glass look will result.

If the spaces between the shapes are very fine it will create a crackle or weblike effect. I have made full color collage paintings this way, sometimes adding paint to sharpen the image.

Or colored papers can be cemented in place and covered with a colored piece of acetate. This transparent layer unifies all the otherwise separate parts.

There are as many ways to make a collage as there are artists, so experiment all the time. Many great ideas are the result of accidents, even mistakes. By correcting something that went wrong, a whole new way of working can be reached. The only way to know in advance what a material or color combination will do is to have done it many times before. The most accidental tearing of a shape will, with practice, become an accepted part of your expression.

ALPHABETICAL ABSTRACTION   *Oscar Liebman*   Combination of two- and three- dimensional elements

Then, if you are under pressure to deliver a job, you will have
a large choice of methods from which to choose and good
craftsmanship will become second nature. Keep experimenting
and keep learning.

THREE-DIMENSIONAL EFFECTS

IN NEW YORK CITY the street number of a certain building takes the form of a ten-foot-high metal image, which stands before its entrance like a monumental piece of sculpture. This is only the latest use of alphabetical and numerical forms, known as super graphics, that are sculptured in the round rather than painted or carved.

Graphic design is based upon the proper use of type styles. The right choice of type can even increase the meaning of a series of words. Think of the words "speed," "slow," "high," "fat," and imagine the meaning of each word expressed by the letters with which they are spelled. This kind of graphic thinking is a type of visual poetry. The basis of this expressive lettering is time. Most advertising tries to capture attention and get its message across as rapidly as possible. Everything on the page must carry as much expressive weight as possible.

Raised type is a relief form that makes a strong contribution to the impact of the message. These letters can be in different materials, such as plastic, wood, plaster, or metal. You can even design and cut out your own letters. See the facing page for a picture of a collage made solely from letters.

Personally, I use a plastic alphabet that comes in different type faces. Sometimes you can find wood or metal letters while browsing in flea markets or bazaars. Store them for future use so they will be handy when the right time comes along.

When I need something more distinctive, I create my own. I find acrylic modeling paste right for my needs. Of course other materials can be used equally well. Some artists prefer plaster, clay, wood, or metal. I make each letter by building up a thin coat, letting it dry, then applying the next layer until the right height is reached. It can be further refined, shaped, and given texture and color as is appropriate for the job.

With three-dimensional work, as with that worked on a flat surface, it is most important to find a style that reflects your own nature. Once you are secure in the natural ability to consistently express yourself as an individual, you can make your work as varied as possible, and not worry about losing your graphic identity. See pages 37-40 for color reproductions of two- and three-dimensional collages.

You must learn to think in 3-D until this extension in space becomes a natural way to function. Just as a brush is strange until its use is mastered, so it is with working in dimension.

Don't be afraid to use a lot of brightly colored objects. They can be toned down, or grayed slightly to keep them in place. This is just visual editing.

Two-dimensional vs. Three-dimensional

Perhaps examples that range from a flat collage to a three-dimensional collage will be helpful.

I had to do an illustration that spread across two pages. To set the scene, I used a loose pen drawing that was fairly busy. Then I inserted a small piece of a photograph of a girl's head. As small as this was, it jumped out and commanded attention. It set up a strong visual contrast that was exactly right for the title of the story: "What's a Nice Girl Like You Doing In a Place Like This?" (See pages 84 and 85.)

The next example moves out into 3-D. It was an ad for a bottle of scotch. On the label it stated that it was produced by "appointment" of several kings of England. What could be more natural than to transform the bottle itself into the sculptured figure of a king? I formed the face with acrylic modeling paste right on the neck of the bottle. As this dried, it formed a strong bond to the bottle itself. When the face was refined and all the detail was added, I used buttons, bits of fur, cardboard, costume jewelry, and cloth, and made the eyes from a color reproduction of a photo-

COLLAGE FOR TENNIS BOOK *Oscar Liebman* Combination of two- and three-dimensional elements Permission, Grossett & Dunlop

YORUBA GODS AND HEROES *Oscar Liebman* Construction The bas-relief statue (based on plaques of the Yoruba of Ife — a Nigerian tribe) was made with modeling paste (an acrylic mixture), then the background of bamboo, rattan, and wood was formed and glued into traditional Yoruba designs. The bas-relief was affixed into position and painted to harmonize with the background colors. After the paint and glue dried, the costume jewelry was pasted on and the entire construction glazed over with a polymer medium Permission, Fawcett Publications

HITLER *Oscar Liebman* Sculpture of Hitler and scraps of newspaper and photograph

PRESSURE   *Oscar Liebman*   Combination of two- and three-dimensional elements   Merck, Sharpe & Dohme)

NO FINAL VICTORIES *Fred Otnes* Combination of two-dimensional elements including photographs of political personages, buildings, flag Permission, Ballantine Books Inc.

LIONS AND CUBS *Joseph Veno* Three-dimensional construction Permission, Honeywell Information Systems Inc.

WOODTYPE AND FIGURE OF PRINTER IN 3-D   *Donald M. Hedin*   Construction   Permission, Donald M. Hedin

I CAN SELL YOU ANYTHING   *Gerry Gersten*   Construction combining two- and three-dimensional elements   Permission, Ballantine Books Inc.

SONG OF INDIA   *William Duevell*   Three-dimensional construction for record cover   Permission, ABC Records

WE SET TRENDS   Combination of mixed media   Permission, Braniff International

THE BOTTLE IN 3-D   *Oscar Liebman*   Construction (See page 36 for a description of the author's procedures in creating this collage.)   Hedges & Butler

graph. The entire bottle became the figure of a king, and it was used standing by itself, royally proclaiming the message on the label: "Est. A.D. 1667 in the reign of H.M. King Charles II"! (See the middle figure above.)

With all three-dimensional objects, light and shade add a rich and dramatic quality that is otherwise missing. There is a more intense theatricality that underlines the advertising message.

When papers of very different textures are used as a background, they can be lit in such a way as to make subtle and pleasing contrasts. Try not to choose materials that are perfect in themselves. They tend to jump out and distract attention from the work as a whole.

Sculptured letters can be made to cast long quiet shadows or

MUSTANG '67   *Oscar Liebman*   Two-dimensional collage   Ford Motor Co.

those which are short and harsh. The use of light in photographing a construction is equal to the use of brush in painting.

Black and White

There are times when you must work in black and white. There may not be enough money to pay for a color reproduction. In this case you must be careful to choose material that will carry well in all the tones of gray, ranging from black to white. Since you may prefer to use colored material or objects, it is a good idea to use a photostat of them instead. Then you will be able to add dark and light so that nothing "drops out" or gets lost when it is printed. (See pages 44-48, 64, 95 for examples of collages created in black and white.)

NEW TECHNIQUES IN ILLUSTRATION

C OLLAGE ILLUSTRATION HAS AN IMMEDIATE IMPACT ON CONTEMPORARY SOCIETY because it is based upon the transformation of thrown-off remnants of modern man. All the products and sentiments of yesterday are made to speak of today.

For this reason it is used in newspapers, on book jackets, posters, story illustrations, annual reports, and promotion pieces, and throughout advertising.

The emotional content of this new form ranges from sheer beauty to rasping political comment.

The individual viewpoint of the artist is made more forceful by virtue of the fact that actual concrete objects are used. The object-quality of the finished work transcends subjective expression.

Newspapers

More and more, newspapers are discovering the power of collage design. *Newsday*, of Long Island, New York, uses a great deal of mixed-media collage. *The New York Times* has steadily increased its use of the above in its Sunday Book Review and News of the Week sections. (See pages 44-48.)

Newspaper art is one of the most difficult for the illustrator. The reproduction quality is so poor that it forces severe limitations

BROADWAY BOOM   *George Delmerico*   Two-dimensional collage combining print matter, photographs, and photostats   *The New York Times*

on all art work. A good job must be done in black and white with a minimum of grays or halftones.

Get everything photostated. Try to drop out gray areas so that a high contrast is obtained. Then touch up the stats to make them even more clear. Old line engravings combined with pen and ink read very well with photos.

This combination is evident in the fine illustration on page 46 by Ned Levine, "The Fed: Big Machine That Does."

Bob Newman, on the other hand, uses photostats of represen-

tations of well-known heads of state to illustrate the international chess game of politics. (See page 47.)

In a story about rape, the same artist creates a texture of photographed faces and drawings to catch the theme as well as the attention of the reader. (See page 47.)

In his illustration of the Mideast oil situation as a money squeeze, Warren Weilbacher uses a halftone photograph with great effect. The fist full of money is cut out and placed against a grid made of flags for stark contrast. The flags and the oil well are drawn in line, with a little tone added to solidify the composition. (See page 48.)

THE FED: BIG MACHINE THAT DOES   *Ned Levine*   Two-dimensional collage combining print matter, drawings, and photographs   Permission, *Newsday*

Book Jackets

A book jacket is really a small poster. It must attract the eye of a customer in the midst of a jungle of competing designs. Collage stands out especially in this setting.

The majority of jackets are limited in the use of color. To keep the cost down, only two or three colors are used. (Remember, black is counted as a color.) When colors are reproduced in two or three halftones and superimposed on one another, a rich variety results. It takes experience to visualize all these possibilities.

The use of colored acetate overlays of varied tones has already been described. At this point their use can be really appreciated. Color limitations can be handled very well with their aid.

POLITICAL CHESS GAME *Bob Newman* Two-dimensional collage combining drawing and photographs Permission, *Newsday*

Printed matter and photographs can be photostated, or even xeroxed, if an unusual texture is desired, and the color sheets can be placed over them.

The space you have to work in depends upon the amount and type of lettering that must be included. You can illustrate the location and time period of a story, or use concrete objects if the book has to do with one subject—cooking, for example.

FACES *Bob Newman* Two-dimensional collage combining photographs of faces and drawing Permission, *Newsday*

Mideast Oil: The Money Squeeze

Oil-producing nations in the Mideast are building up surpluses of money—called 'petro-dollars'—from their sales of oil. That worries the U.S. and other industrialized nations, who fear that the Mideastern countries might use their newly acquired dollars to disrupt the economies of the rest of the world. Page 6.

MIDEAST OIL: THE MONEY SQUEEZE   *Warren Weilbacher*   Two-dimensional collage combining photograph and drawing   Permission, *Newsday*

VOYAGES INTO TOMORROW

edited by Robert Hoskins

Stories by
KATHERINE MacCLEAN
BARRY N. MALZBERG
ROBERT SHECKLEY
POUL ANDERSON
ANNE McCAFFREY
C. M. KORNBLUTH
R. A. LAFFERTY
URSULA LeGUIN
JOE L. HENSLEY
HENRY KUTTNER
DEAN R. KOONTZ
AND WILLIAM TENN

THE LIBERATED FUTURE   *Oscar Liebman*   Two-dimensional collage combining a drawing and photograph of man's face   Permission, *Fawcett Publications*

The illustration above, done for Fawcett Publications, was for a science fiction book called *The Liberated Future*. It is composed mainly of art work with a human head pasted on the reflection of the butterfly. This small bit of collage adds a new and surprising dimension that takes the image beyond that of an ordinary butterfly and presents an idea that is ominous and a little terrifying.

This is a good example of the subtle after-image quality of collage when used with imagination. The covers of paperback books are usually small in dimension. For this reason the design must be kept simple so that it will read well. However, for the most part, they are done in full color, and this allows complete freedom in choice of material.

Look at the illustrations in this section and see how much variety of selection works for books.

Illustration in Books, Magazines, Annual Reports, etc.

I have used collage illustrations for chapter headings in books with great success. When there are empty spaces—at the end of a chapter, for instance—art helps set or sustain the mood of the book. It also gives the pages a more interesting look.

One of my most satisfying jobs consisted of doing sixty pieces for an eighth-grade Catholic reader.

Such a large amount of work was not hard to do in itself, except for the requirement that each piece had to have its own individual design. For this I was glad to have a good collection of materials at hand from which to choose. When I couldn't find what I needed, I drew or painted it.

Collage illustrations are very well suited for children. The technique of pasting things together is something that comes from their own experience and they read it with quick understanding.

Another time I was commissioned to do an illustration for one of the condensed books published by *Reader's Digest*. The non-fiction story was about the San Francisco earthquake.

This was a hard problem for me, but it turned out to be perfect for the use of three-dimensional objects. I used burned fragments of wood, rocks, stones, and plaster along with pictures.

I designed it with a lot of empty space around the margin in order to force the main impact to the center. I wanted everything to be crushed and toppling. It worked out very well, and both the art director and I were pleased at how it captured the essence of the story. (See the color plate on page 92.)

In magazine illustration the story must be brought out. These themes can cover all kinds of moods and actions. They can be period pieces, science fiction, mysteries, love and adventure plots, or factual articles on biography, travel, or mathematics.

Advertising is different from the above insofar as you become an artist/salesman for the product. You must stay closer to the actual limitations of the product in order to get across specific points.

Consider the advertising for a Ford car. Television commercials can show it in motion, in combination with people. With collage, the artist must catch subtle nuances that are not visible on the TV screen. The art must work with type-set copy, but if smiles and gestures were superimposed on the ad it could show how enjoyable it is to own a Ford. The fact that all different types of people love Ford cars can also be shown by collage in a rich, pictorial way. (See the reproduction on page 42.)

Related to advertisements are annual reports and various promotion pieces.

Annual reports are sent to stockholders to show them the state

HEAD OF CHRIST   *Oscar Liebman*   Two-dimensional collage combining drawing, printed matter, and photographs (Illustration for book *God's Saving Presence*)   Benzinger Bros.

of the company. They are often done in full color on good paper, especially by large companies, as self-promotion, to signify that all is well and growing. The actual contents are usually dry outlines of what has been done and how, along with hard business figures and charts. Illustration design is needed to lighten the "story" and to make it attractive.

I designed a report of this type for the twenty-fifth anniversary of Weight Watchers. In an attempt to symbolize their method of fighting obesity, I found a picture of an overweight man and made his head from one of their buttons on which was printed the slogan "Fight Obesity." Unfortunately, they didn't like the idea; they wanted a before-and-after image that would underline their program.

Since this was not the first time I've had to please a corporate group, I was not too surprised. I rethought the problem and came up with a new solution.

I left the overweight fellow on the front cover and continued the design around to the back. Here I made a grouping of their products. On top of some photographs I cut an actual box from their cottage cheese and glued it on as if it were being pushed through the board from the back. When this was lit a shadow was cast across the composition that dramatically tied everything together.

In another assignment I was given an illustration to do with no accompanying script. My instructions were to conceive a picture to sum up the era 1960-70. It was a challenge that resulted in a harsh collage filled with the idea of the assassinations, riots, anti-Vietnam feelings and general upheaval. I called it "The Violent '60's."

Posters

A poster attempts to attract attention in the shortest amount of time. It must be simple to read and have a hard-hitting image. This doesn't mean that there is no room for subtle qualities; but the dominant force behind poster usage must be respected. Fast impact comes first; then the secondary parts can be allowed their own space. I like to float the collage on a large one-color background. That leaves room for the lettering and adds strength to the visual message.

Examples of Collage Illustration

The collages gathered in this book represent the work of practicing commerial artists. Most of today's successful illus-

A SALUTE TO GLENN MILLER　*Oscar Liebman*　Two- and three-dimensional collage for a record album　Metro Records

BROADWAY POSTER   *Oscar Liebman*   Combination of two- and three-dimensional elements

trators use collage—some more frequently than others. The list is long; it includes Peter Max, Milton Glaser, Tom Daly, Bob Peak, Barbara Nessim, Ted Colonosis, Len Berzofsky, the artists whose works are reproduced in this book, and of course many others. Since it was impossible to reproduce the work of every fine illustrator, I had to select a few that I felt would reflect individual expression in the use of materials and in the solution of very precise commissions.

Look at each one with care and try to appreciate the thought that went into each work. They are meant to inspire you with your own ideas and to indicate the immense scope of this new creative activity:

Alan Cober

Alan Cober has used collage for book illustration and advertising. He is an award-winning artist whose work has been exhibited in museums around the country. The reproductions below and on page 56 are from a series of collages he created for CONOCO 74, a promotional publication of Continental Oil Company.

THREE COWBOYS   *Alan Cober*   Drawing with photographs of faces pasted on drawn figures of cowboys   Permission, Continental Oil Co.

MEMORY OF A WILD RANCH (detail)   *Alan Cober*   Drawing and photostat of building
Permission, Continental Oil Co.

Sam Fischer

While in Rome on a Fulbright grant, this artist became interested in the texture of ordinary wrapping paper used in food shops. He became completely absorbed in creating pictures from paper and pigment. Using a variety of papers to build up a low relief image of strong texture, he has created a unique collage style.

Fischer will make his own paper if necessary, using a kitchen blender to form the pulp.

When Mead Paper wanted someone to present the searching spirit of their paper line, Sam Fischer was the obvious choice.

THE HORIZONS OF MEAD I   *Sam Fischer*   Papers and drawing   Permission, Mead Corporation

THE HORIZONS OF MEAD II (detail)   *Sam Fischer*   Papers and drawing   Permission, Mead   Corporation

Louis S. Glanzman

A fine draftsman, Glanzman is known for his ability to work in any medium, from line drawing to full color.

The covers for *Time* magazine reveal his control as well as his imagination. What doesn't show is the tremendous pressure that this type of publication exerts on the artist. The cover story has to break and be on the newsstands practically the same week.

Collage is perfect for this high-pressure work, since it saves so much drawing or painting time.

In the cover below of *Time* magazine showing a student strike at Harvard, a photo of a statue of the university's founder is glazed with color and placed against a background of xeroxed photos of dissatisfied students. The gray tone of the photos serves to set the stage for the story as well as to set off the title of the magazine.

STRIKE HARVARD   *Louis S. Glanzman*   Photograph, Xerox copies of prints   *Time*

Fred Otnes

An award-winning collage artist, Fred Otnes has worked for such clients as *Fortune*, *Life*, *Seventeen*, *McCalls*, RCA, ABC-TV, American Airlines, and AT&T.

His work is characterized by an unusual spatial quality. It is not so much the use of three-dimensional objects along with bits of posters, photos, type, etc., but a special way of glazing all these

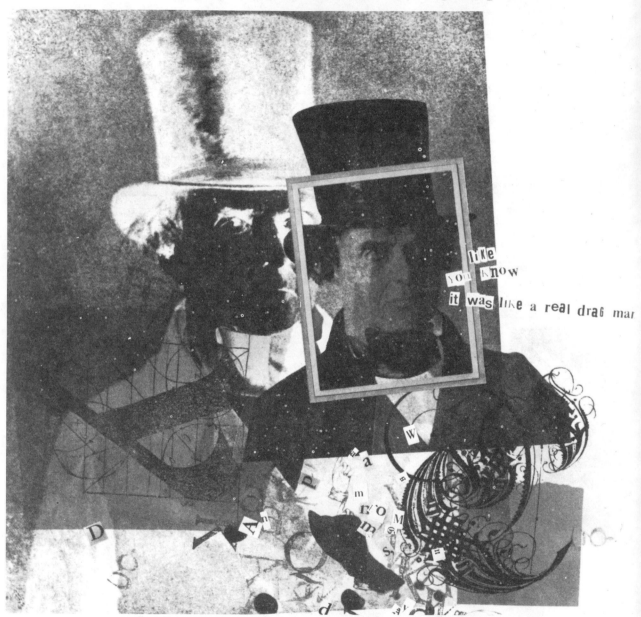

SPEECH PATTERNS   *Fred Otnes*   Two-dimensional collage combining photographs, photoprints, type   (Created for publicity booklet "Commentaries")   Permission, ABC Television

parts down so that the main image floats clearly to the front of the picture space. See also the reproduction of work by Otnes on the color plate on page 39.

What might seem a haphazard collection of items join together to form a powerful design.

VIEW FROM LOUISIANA *Fred Otnes* Two-dimensional collage combining drawing, photographs of figures and objects (Created for publicity booklet "Commentaries") Permission, ABC Television

WILLIAM EDDY   *Fred Otnes*   Two-dimensional collage with prints and photostats   Permission, *Creative Living*, Caldwell Communications

Tom Upshur

In order to bring out the central theme of a story, Upshur utilizes the widest range of technical abilities. He can work in a broad Expressionistic style, with a hard, clean edge, or do soft airbrush renderings. Because of this facility, his work can be used across the whole spectrum of the graphic communications market. Reproductions of Upshur's works appear below, and on pages 64, 83, 87, 95, 100, and on the color plate on page 89.

LIFE   *Tom Upshur*   Construction   Harcourt, Brace, Jovanovich   Permission, Tom Upshur

BLACK FIGHTING MEN   *Tom Upshur*   Two-dimensional collage combining photographs and news pictures   Lothrop, Lee, Shepard Co.

Theresa Fasolino

The outstanding quality of this artist's work is the physical use of three dimensions. Teri Fasolino, aside from being a painter and collagist, is a constructionist. In her illustration for *Everyman an Inventor* she has used actual objects contained in a boxlike room, where collage and painting are heightened by real light and shade. The result is a highly individual solution to a problem in illustration.

EVERYMAN AN INVENTOR   *Theresa Fasolino*   Construction combining two- and three- dimensional elements   *Creative Living*   Permission, Theresa Fasolino

Gerald McConnell

Since 1953 McConnell has been doing free-lance illustration. Originally known for his pencil drawings, he now uses both collage and constructions, for which he has won many awards.

His studio contains a carpenter's workbench and a storage area complete with objects from antiquity and collections of all types of things for use in his constructions. His favorite artist, not surprisingly, is Joseph Cornell.

CONGLOMERATE   *Gerald McConnell*   Construction   Celanese Corporation

SMILE *Gerald McConnell* Construction Permission, Eastern Air Lines Incorporated

MODERN TIMES *Gerald McConnell* Construction A. T. & T.

Ann Dalton

The reproductions of the collages on this and the facing page were done for Fawcett Books by Ann Dalton. She uses three-dimensional constructions made of plastic sheets. The objects included are symbolic of the contents of the story. They were chosen with great care so that their meaning would first attract the potential reader and then pique his curiosity.

TRANSFORMATIONS I   *Ann Dalton*   Construction   Permission, Fawcett Publications

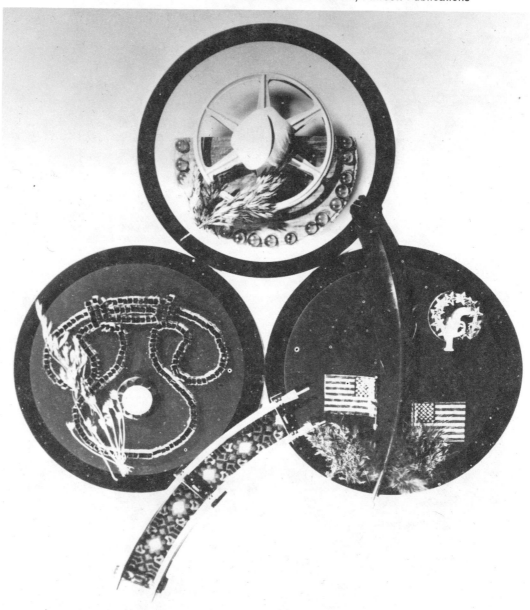

TRANSFORMATIONS II   *Ann Dalton*   Construction   Permission, Fawcett Publications

MAN AND NATURE   *François Colos*   Two-dimensional collage combining drawing and old prints   Permission, *Creative Living*, Caldwell Communications

BUCKMINSTER FULLER   *Ritchie Kiehl/Artspeak*   Two-dimensional collage combining photograph, drawing, old prints, and handwritten notes   Permission, *The American Way,* Caldwell Communications

SAN FRANCISCO EARTHQUAKE I *Oscar Liebman* Construction combining two- and three-dimensional elements   Reader's Digest Condensed Books

A COLLAGE
IN THE
MAKING

A T THIS POINT you might find it informative to follow the step-by-step sequence from the receipt of a commission to the delivery of the finished collage.

I was given a script that concerned Watergate and President Nixon. After reading it carefully, I let my imagination play with a flood of ideas. The sudden force of this event struck everyone with hammer-like blows. The print and electronic media were blasting every detail of this momentous happening fact by fact.

I thought of an image of Nixon that would express the fact that he was still "stonewalling," or putting his best face forward as if nothing were going on despite the continuous revelations, tapes, etc.

This suggested a bas-relief of Nixon's head jutting through all of the surrounding turmoil. Once the basic idea crystallized, I had to gather all the background materials needed. I went over to the corner of the studio dubbed "the junk yard" by my *very* understanding wife. It is filled with old newspapers, magazines, clippings, and odds and ends. The few things I feel are missing I buy from various sources.

Since I had a little time before my deadline, I carefully searched and sorted through all my material. I soon had a stack of things about three feet high. There is just no way to get around this

A Corner of the Author's Studio

laborious process. It is the first essential step in editing out the material that will fit as opposed to less appropriate or duplicate items. It was of the utmost importance that only those things be used that would make a total, searing statement.

After the three-foot pile had dwindled to a mere two feet, my board was packed with usable material along with paints, glues, brushes, cutting tools, and everything else that collage demands. I felt like I was in the center of a walled fortress!

Since I had a strong idea of what I wanted to do, I made a rough sketch of the way it would look.

Every job must be sketched out a few times so that the compositional parts can be tested and made to work together. These sketches are called "comps," short for "comprehensives." Each artist works differently, even in this early period of representation. Some use very simple, abstract shapes; others supply a more finished idea. These "comps" are then taken to the art director for approval.

If the sketch is the same size as the original and is fairly detailed, it can be traced right onto the board as a guide for the finished work. In this way it will resemble the original sketch that was approved by the art director.

In the present case, I did some quick sketches and the relief of the head of Nixon. I took these to the art director, and after some suggestions and minor changes I got his OK.

Going back to my "walled fortress," I prepared my work area. Most commerical art is done larger than the original so that it sharpens and picks up a more detailed look when reduced and printed. I prefer not to work more than three times as large as the original because the newspaper material I use can lose quality when it is reduced.

Author in Studio

A COLLAGE IN THE MAKING I

Once the right area is sketched on the board, I gesso the board with acrylic gesso. Since each coat will dry in ten minutes or so it does not take long to get the board smooth and workable.

Then I make a few simple lines on the board that echo the layout shown the art director. Don't let these lines bind you, since new ideas may come along that will add to the composition.

The photographs that show me at work were taken by David Howard, an established photographer. He said I looked like a jumping jack as I moved back and forth from the pile of material to the board. The truth is that I was so intent on filling that flat white surface that I forgot he was in the room!

The few shots of me at work give the barest indication of all the shuffling back and forth of material—fitting things together, trying textures against one another, using touches of color for mood and depth, and just getting things set without losing the excitement I wanted.

A COLLAGE IN THE MAKING II

A COLLAGE IN THE MAKING III

A COLLAGE IN THE MAKING IV

A COLLAGE IN THE MAKING V

By this time my deadline was approaching, so I used rubber cement on paper areas because this permits the paper to be moved around easily until the correct place for each is found.

For glazing, a gloss acrylic medium was used. This medium is both a binding agent and a protective varnish.

Lastly, the tapes and the head of Nixon were bonded to the board with a glue-all. I used a color overlay called Color Tex over the news photos of Nixon's associates as well as over the banner headlines. This type of overlay allows a color change without loss of legibility.

The collage, now complete, when printed, reproduced with strength and clarity, as you can see on the following page, and in full color on page 91 as it was actually published.

COMPLETED COLLAGE: NIXON AND THE TAPES *Oscar Liebman*

MARKETING SUGGESTIONS

THE ILLUSTRATION FIELD IS ONE OF HURRIED DEADLINES, frustrations of all kinds, late payments, acrimonious and sometimes unpleasant relationships with publishers and art directors. But for all of this it can be one of the most satisfying and wholesome ways of making a living through self-expression. In other words, earning money and gaining self-satisfaction at the same time is an art in itself.

Preparing a Portfolio

To begin with, you need samples. This means that you must gather together a group of work in various media for different types of jobs. Collages, and particularly constructions, can be heavy and bulky to carry around. You should have at least six pieces of work. If you only carry photographic transparency slides it simplifies the problem but it does not make the same impression. It is always important to show actual art work. Slides will allow you to demonstrate your dexterity and range of work, while originals point out the actual creativity of the work itself.

So it is best to compromise. Carry one or two originals of your best work, and then fill in with slides. Remember, it is better to have a few really good things than a lot of medium-quality collages. In this case, less is more, for the uninspired work can take away from your best efforts. It is very difficult to judge one's own

MARKET PLACE   *Oscar Liebman*   Two-dimensional collage consisting of type, bits of newsprint, magazine and directory logos, and drawing   (Created by the author as an illustration for this chapter)

COLLAGE FOR A FOURTH-GRADE READER   *Tom Upshur*   Combination of two- and three-dimensional elements including rice and wire   Silver Burdett

work. If you know a professional, ask him or her to help you pick that which best represents your own style. These artists are, on the whole, happy to help one of their kind.

Next it is important to find companies that use art work sympathetic to your talent and point of view. Look at everything you can find in magazines, books, trade journals, and posters in order to find a frame of reference into which your work will fit. Study all the illustrative material you can find and then research the names of the publishers, agencies, etc.

In the public library you will find a listing of advertising agencies, promotion houses, trade publications, publishing houses, and editorial outlets in a reference book called the *Stan-*

WHAT'S A NICE GIRL LIKE YOU DOING IN A PLACE LIKE THIS?   *Oscar Liebman*   Drawing and photograph of girl's head *The American Way,* Caldwell Comunications

dard Directory of Advertising Agencies. This is updated each year to include the names of active art directors and editors. Make up a list of those you feel would be interested in seeing your work. Call them for an appointment.

Telephoning is a vital part of making connections for jobs. Since there usually is a waiting period between your call and the appointment, make a lot of calls. Go from one to another.

Your samples should be as presentable as possible. Have them matted and clean looking. You will also need a card with your telephone number, just in case you make a good impression!

Don't be afraid to arrive a little early for an appointment. This will give you a chance to look the place over. Many reception rooms have art work on the walls that have been used in publications.

If the art director seems to be doing eighteen things while looking at your samples, pay attention. All these distractions can also reveal aspects of the job from which you can profit.

Be careful not to oversell the samples of your work; let them speak for themselves. Later you can ask questions and find out how you stand in the estimation of the editor or art director. Learn from criticism. It is not necessarily directed at you personally; it is more likely to be an explanation of what a particular company wants and needs. If you really want to move into that specific area, listen carefully. Do not be afraid to ask if they know of someone else who might like to see your work. This can lead to a good connection, one that would otherwise remain unknown to you.

After an interview you may be asked to leave a sample of your work for their files. The best and least expensive way to do this is to have full-color photographic prints of your best work imprinted with your name, address, and phone number. They are postcard size and serve as both card and sample.

After you have had a few commissions you will be able to get extra proofs that you can use in your portfolio and leave for samples.

THE SALESMAN *Oscar Liebman* Construction combining drawing, newsprint, picture of a dollar bill, and assorted merchandise

THE PACKAGING DILEMMA *Tom Upshur* Construction Permission, Tom Upshur

However, you must learn that all samples are not the same. Do not leave a sample of advertising art at a book publishing house. They prefer you to present them with an idea of how your art will work on a page with type. The successful blending of story and picture is their aim.

A knowledge of color separation, the limitations of budget, and an understanding of deadlines is particularly appreciated by editors.

A 'pilgrim of peace' enters

ST. PAUL   *Oscar Liebman*   Two-dimensional collage combining drawing, bits of newsprint, and pictures of people (illustration for book *God's Saving Presence*)   Benzinger Bros.

MADONNA AND TRAINS *Tom Upshur* Construction Permission, Tom Upshur

GENERAL RELATIVITY *Steven Karchin* Pencil drawing on brown paper with photo prints on lithographic film paper Permission, Steven Karchin

THE PRINCE'S BRIDE *Peter Roth* Construction Permission, Ballantine Books Inc.

BASEBALL HEROES   *Oscar Liebman*   Combination of two- and three-dimensional elements, Grossett & Dunlop

WOMAN WITH DOG *Steven Karchin* Construction combining two- and three-dimensional elements: oil painting, wooden strips, dried flowers, and miscellaneous memorabilia Permission, Steven Karchin

DIRTY BLUES BAND *William Duevell* Collage for record cover Permission, ABC Records

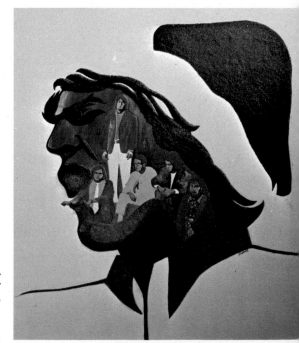

NIXON AND THE TAPES *Oscar Liebman* Combination of two- and three-dimensional elements (See chapter "Collage in the Making")

SAN FRANCISCO EARTHQUAKE II   *Oscar Liebman*   Construction combining two- and three-dimensional elements   Reader's Digest Condensed Books

Samples for advertising editors must underline the relationship of the art to a product. It must leap out of the page and grasp the reader's attention. The same holds true for book jackets and paperback book covers. Color plates on pages 89 through 92 show a good mix of two- and three-dimensional collages and subject matter for a portfolio of samples.

Specialized publications are a good market for collage. If you go to *Seventeen* magazine, for example, be sure you show things that would be of interest to teenagers. Subjects such as music, clothes, decorating ideas, and fictional matter that deals with this age group are all integral to this magazine's makeup.

If you have nothing in your portfolio that fits this kind of magazine, make up a few things to show as samples. Study each publication thoroughly and see what ideas you can come up with. This is the only way to break into new markets. If collage has not been used in a particular area, the time might just be ripe for your samples to click!

It is important to be consistent in your work. The most successful illustrators have a certain look to their art that gives it an identity. Once this stylistic quality is reached, you can vary your ideas and materials without losing the individual feeling of your

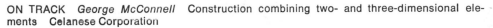

ON TRACK *George McConnell* Construction combining two- and three-dimensional elements Celanese Corporation

MAE WEST   *Oscar Liebman*   Combination of drawing with two- and three-dimensional elements   Author's collection

work. Each job offers a different outlook, and yet your own hand-writing must show through.

Many art directors do not even make a layout until they have seen the illustration. Then, and only then, do they allot a place for the type, book title, body copy, or logos, depending on the job.

The next most important factor is time. In most cases the work is due "yesterday"! When you consider the enormous amount of talent readily available to the art director in his time of need, you can picture your competition.

I have worked around the clock on many occasions, as have a lot of illustrators I know.

Two- or three-dimensional collage is, in fact, a time saver. It gives you an edge over hand-rendering objects and saves everyone time. In addition, the result has an emotional power that fits commercial markets to perfection.

POVERTY *Tom Upshur* Drawing, newsprint, photographs *Business Week*

How to Find a Market

The most difficult thing is getting your work seen. If no one sees your collages, your creative illustrations will remain unused.

There are agents for commercial artists. A good agent, who will represent you well and secure commissions, is as hard to find as an art director who loves your work. There are many agents who are loaded down with twenty or thirty artists. They cannot represent each in a competent manner.

Another type of agent is one who has a studio and contracts the whole job, from layout to type, paste ups, lettering, retouching, and illustrations. This is called a "packaged job," and the agent, acting as art director and designer, splits the commission for the entire work with the artist.

This type of total assignment can include mailing pieces, posters, books, brochures, and even whole magazines. The agent is a kind of free-lance art department for companies that do not

PORTUGAL   *Fred Otnes*   Two-dimensional collage   Permission, Caldwell Communications

have a permanent setup of this kind. Working with such packaged jobs is an invaluable source of experience.

Even when you have work on your table that is due, you must still take time to set up additional appointments. It can be very nerve-wracking to wait around to show your portfolio to an art director when you already have work waiting to be done. How-

FIFTH OF NOVEMBER   *Cliff Condak*   Two- and three-dimensional elements
Permission, Ballantine Books Inc.

ever, there is no other way to keep things flowing. Once you are
really busy with assignments you will be able to get a good agent
to represent you.

At the very beginning you can visit the public library and
check through the *Literary Market Place*. This is a directory of
American book publishers that lists the types of books published

SUPER CARTON   (Artist not identified)   Photographs, postage stamps pasted on sheet music
Permission, Potlatch Packaging

by each of them, gives their addresses and telephone numbers and the names of their editors and art directors. Magazines which sometimes buy illustrations are also listed.

While at the library, go through books that are illustrated. Make a note of the names of publishers who make use of work comparable to yours. In this way you will build a marketing guide that is geared for you. Each of these publishers can be checked, in turn, in the *Literary Market Place*.

The Standard Directory of Advertisers is another fine reference book potentially of great value to the artist in search of a market. It is published by the same company that produces *The Standard Directory of Advertising Agencies* (see pages 83 and

EXPLORING OUR NATION'S HISTORY *Oscar Liebman* Collage for a book cover combining photographs, newsprint, headlines, historical pictures, portraits, and three-dimensional elements   Permission, Globe Book Company

84). The latter lists advertising agencies, their accounts, the names of their art directors or art buyers, and their addresses and telephone numbers. The former lists corporations and businesses which use advertising. Here you will find the names of corporate

WRATH OF GOD   *Tom Upshur*   Two-dimensional collage combining, painting, drawing, and photoprint   **Doubleday**

One of the first man-made fibers produced in America was acetate. Celanese invented it. Today we also make Arnel triacetate, Fortrel polyester, Nylon 66, rayon, and in Canada, polypropylene. More than a billion pounds a year.

THE NEW LINE   *Dave Passalequa*   Photograph and drawing   Celanese Corporation

advertising directors who often do their own promotional work for brochures, direct mailing pieces, annual reports, instruction booklets, and posters. In dealing directly with corporations you have the advantage of having a whole group of public relations work built around your art.

Also examine (if you can lay your hands on any) collections of so-called "house organs"—magazines printed especially for the particular companies. These, like annual reports, are usually well printed on good paper and in full color. They represent a creative as well as a lucrative market for collage art. The only way of getting copies of these house organs may be to write to the public-relations departments of the large commercial and industrial firms.

GENERAL STORE *Steven Karchin* Combination of two- and three-dimensional elements; real window frame and constructed siding of store form foundation over which oil painting illustrates figures and lettering. Original antiques make up window. Permission, *Steven Karchin*

The Madison Avenue Handbook is another valuable directory that lists advertising agencies and art studios all over the country. It will also help you to locate sources for props, old engravings, and models to be photographed for your collage.

The last and most simple directory is the yellow pages of the telephone book. Many ideas for potential markets can be gleaned here.

Slanting Your Work

Slant your work to suit the market. Collages, for example, for *Argosy*, a magazine for men, should obviously be directed toward masculine taste. Think of westerns, war, sports, cars, planes, science fiction, mystery, and action stories in general. An in-depth study of this magazine reveals just what to present to the editor.

CHANGING AFRICA   *Oscar Liebman*   Painting and bits of photographs   Permission, Fawcett Publications

Naturally, you don't want to bring in duplicates of the work already being published. You must research a little and create a new point of view that will best be served by two- or three-dimensional collage. Women's magazines, similarly, present another point of view.

Fortune magazine, and others, like it, lean towards corporate business affairs. Here you must consider such subjects as raw materials, transportation, industrial plants, marketing, and packaging.

The same kind of analysis must be applied to periodicals that are concerned with advertising and promotion.

When you have made an initial contact with an editor or art director, follow up by calling once a month. Make another appointment to show more of your work. If you have proofs of work that has been used, your professional reputation will rise.

Such follow-up appointments can also show how you have listened to advice and leaned your work in the direction of that editor's or director's particular needs.

Along the same line you can send a mailing to each art director you have seen, especially if you can include printed work that has been sold.

The only way you will make a vivid impression is to keep putting your work under the scrutiny of the art director.

A Final Word

The techniques and illustrations in this book are meant to encourage and inspire young illustrators who have not experienced the vast new territory of two- and three-dimensional collage.

There simply is no power or beauty to equal the physical relationship of objects that are given extra reality by actual light and shade. The entire range of color, texture, and spatial dimensions is open to the communications media in a wholly new and contemporary way.

Go out and transform the world!

INDEX